Living LARGE

A Shark's Life

Sara Antill

PowerKiDS press.
New York

For Dominick Riley Rafuls

Published in 2012 by The Rosen Publishing Group, Inc.
29 East 21st Street, New York, NY 10010

First Edition

Editor: Jennifer Way
Book Design: Greg Tucker

Photo Credits: Cover Stephen Frink/Getty Images; pp. 4, 6 (bottom), 7, 8, 12 (top, bottom), 13, 14 (bottom), 15 (top, bottom), 16, 18, 19, 20 Shutterstock.com; p. 5 Visuals Unlimited, Inc./Andy Murch/Getty Images; p. 6 (top) Jeffrey L. Rotman/Time Life Pictures/Getty Images; p. 10 Gary Bell/Getty Images; p. 11 (top) Daniel Gotshall/Getty Images; p. 11 (bottom) David Fleetham/Visuals Unlimited, Inc./Getty Images; p. 14 (top) © Andre Seale/age fotostock; p. 17 Frank Krahmer/Getty Images; p. 21 Brandon Cole/Getty Images; p. 22 Brian Skerry/National Geographic/Getty Images.

Library of Congress Cataloging-in-Publication Data

Antill, Sara.
A shark's life / by Sara Antill. — 1st ed.
p. cm. — (Living large)
Includes index.
ISBN 978-1-4488-4981-9 (library binding) — ISBN 978-1-4488-5110-2 (pbk.) —
ISBN 978-1-4488-5111-9 (6-pack)
1. Sharks—Juvenile literature. I. Title. II. Series.
QL638.9.A577 2012
597.3—dc22

2010053109

Manufactured in the United States of America

CPSIA Compliance Information: Batch #WS11PK: For Further Information contact Rosen Publishing, New York, New York at 1-800-237-9932

Contents

Meet the Shark

From the moment a shark is born, it must take care of itself. As the young shark gets older, its body grows bigger. Someday, the shark will likely have babies of its own. The different stages of life that an animal passes through are called its **life cycle**.

Many people are afraid of sharks. They may have seen movies or read stories about sharks

The tiger shark, shown here, is one of the hundreds of different kinds of sharks.

attacking people. However, shark attacks on people are very uncommon. As scientists study sharks, they learn more and more about these large, fearsome fish. Let's find out more about the life of a shark!

Sharks go through many changes throughout their life cycle. These are young Port Jackson sharks swimming near the coast of Australia.

Big Fish, Small Fish

Not all sharks look the same. There are about 460 different **species** of sharks. The smallest is the dwarf lantern shark. It grows to be only about 7 inches (18 cm) long. The largest shark is the whale shark. It grows to be from 40 to 50 feet (12–15 m)

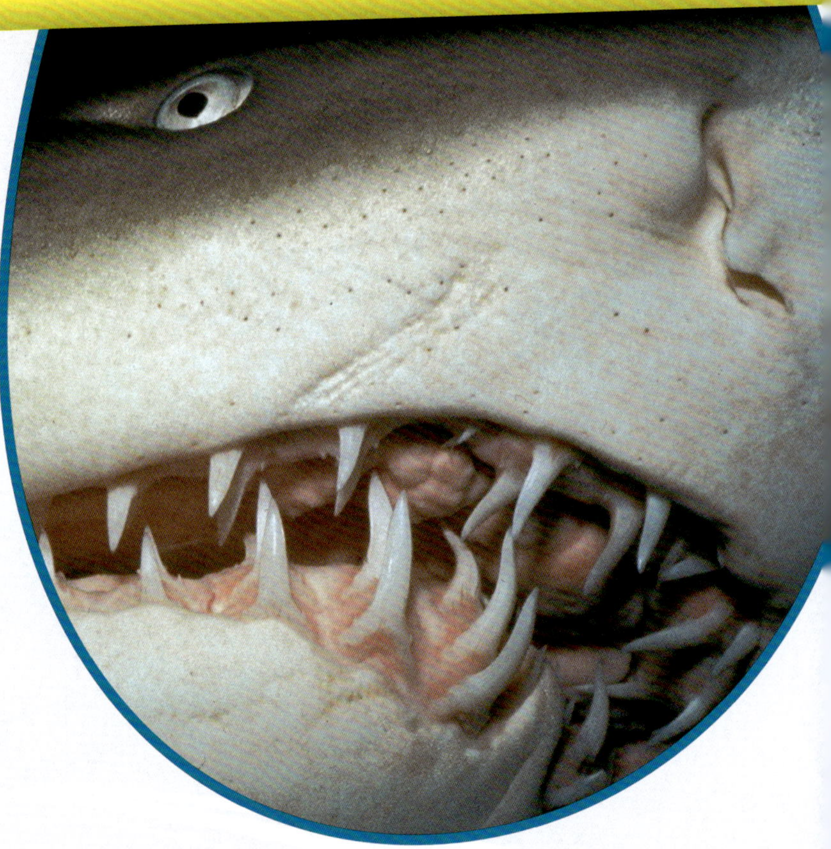

Top: The sand tiger shark is known for its rows of jagged teeth. You can see its teeth even when its mouth is closed! *Left*: The markings on its fins give the blacktip reef shark its name.

long and can weigh more than 20 tons (18 t). The whale shark is not only the biggest shark. It is also the biggest fish in the ocean!

Sharks come in different colors, too. Blue sharks get their name from their blue skin. Whale sharks have white spots on their gray and brown skin.

The whale shark has a wide mouth that it uses to bring in food as it swims.

A Home in the Ocean

Sharks live in oceans all around the world. Some kinds of sharks, such as bull sharks, live in shallow waters. Bull sharks like to swim in places where freshwater and salt water mix. This type of water is called **brackish**. Other sharks, such as sleeper sharks, live in much deeper water. A sleeper shark can live in water as deep as 1,800 feet (550 m).

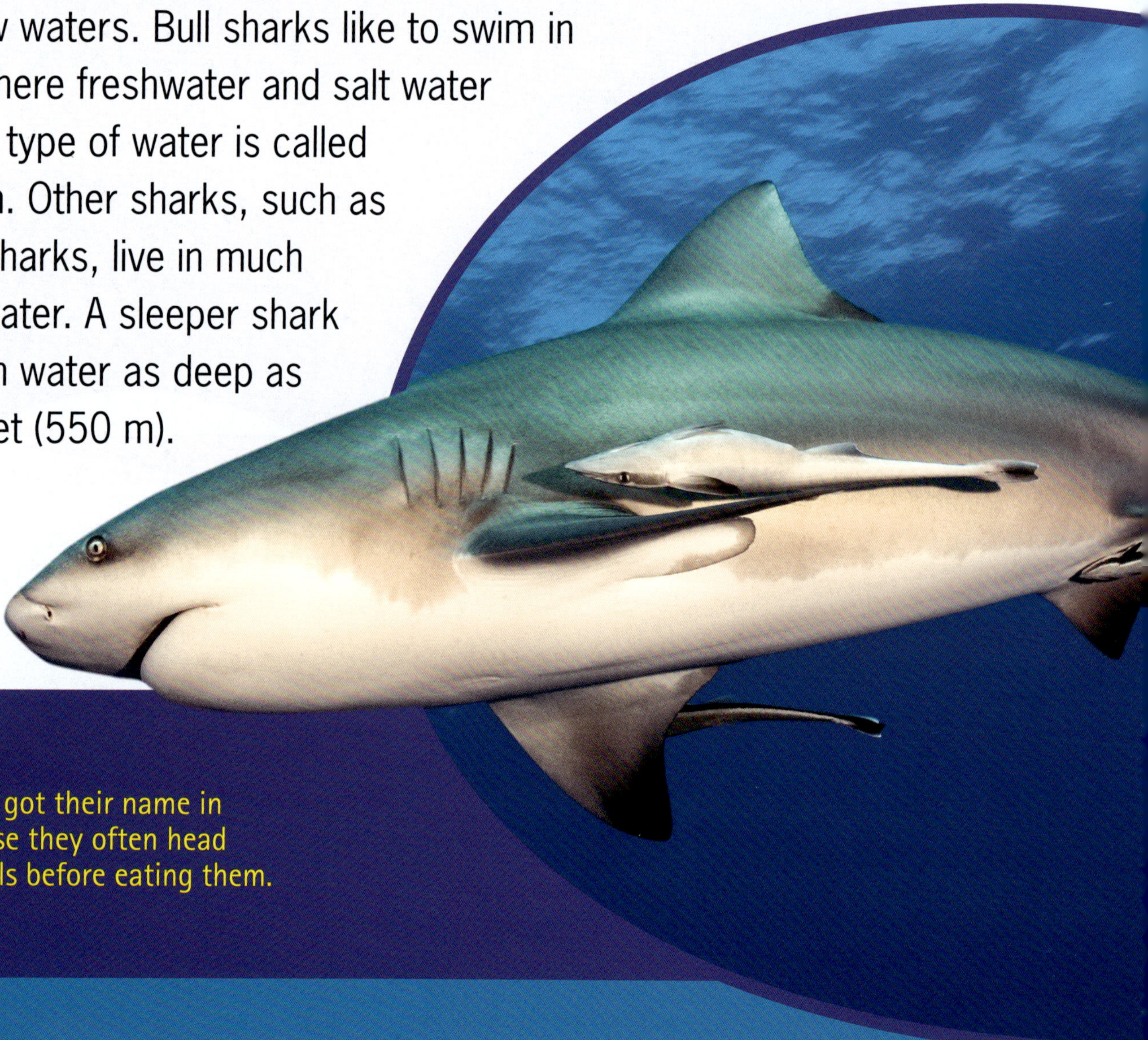

Bull sharks got their name in part because they often head butt animals before eating them.

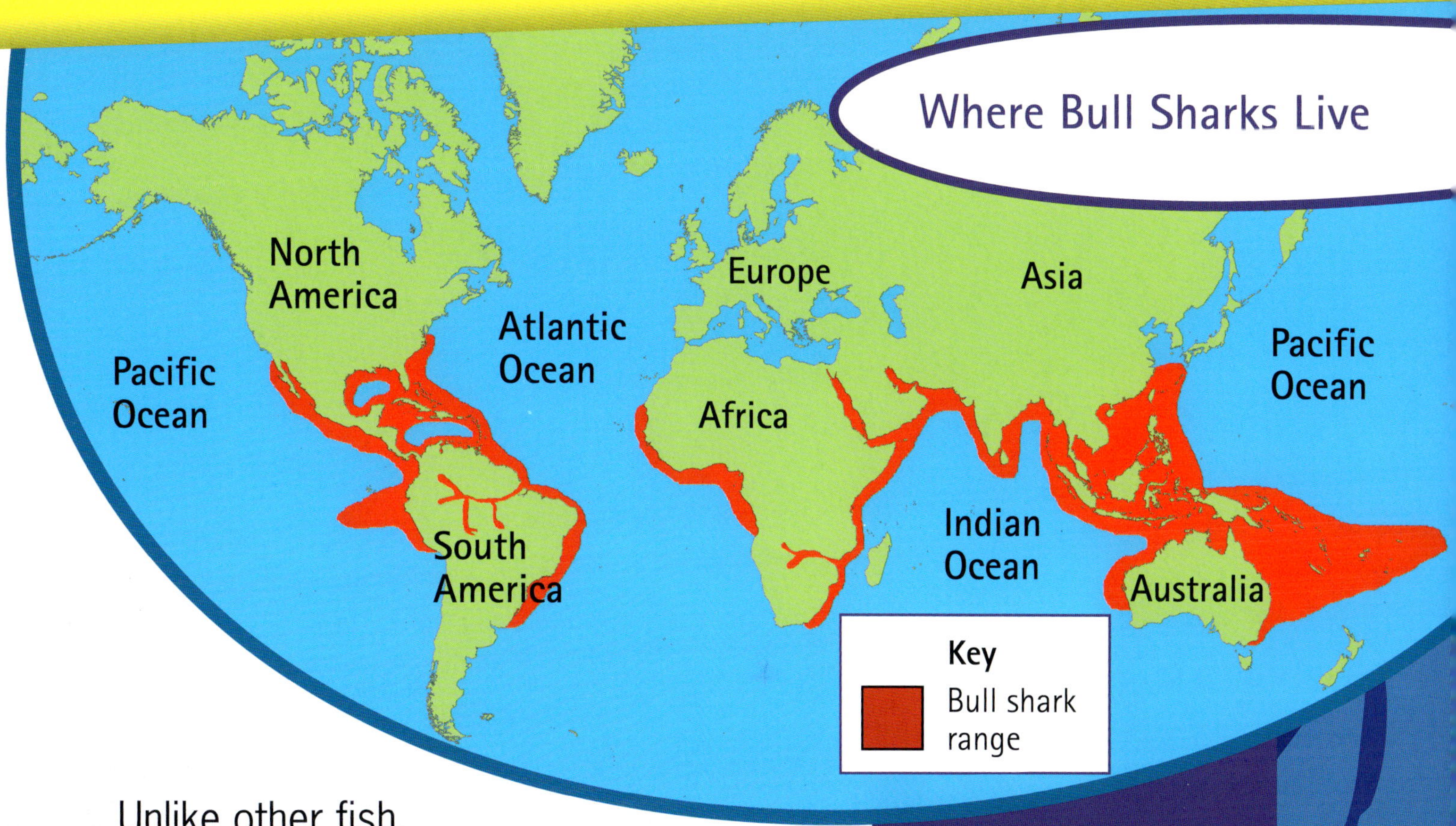

This map shows the bull shark's range in red.

Unlike other fish, sharks do not have any bones. Their bodies are made of **cartilage**. This lets sharks move their bodies in many different directions. It also makes them lighter and able to move quickly.

Finding Food

The whale shark, shown here, swims with its mouth open to catch plankton and small fish. The water goes back out of their gills. This is called filter feeding.

Sharks are **carnivores**. However, different sharks eat different animals. Some, such as the whale shark, swim through the ocean with their mouths open. Small fish and **plankton** get caught in their mouths, while the water is pushed out through their gills.

Some sharks wait for their food to come to them. Angel sharks lie on the ocean floor and eat small fish and **mollusks** that pass by. Other sharks, such as the great white shark, hunt for their food. They use their sharp teeth to tear animals, such as sea lions and seals, into pieces they can swallow.

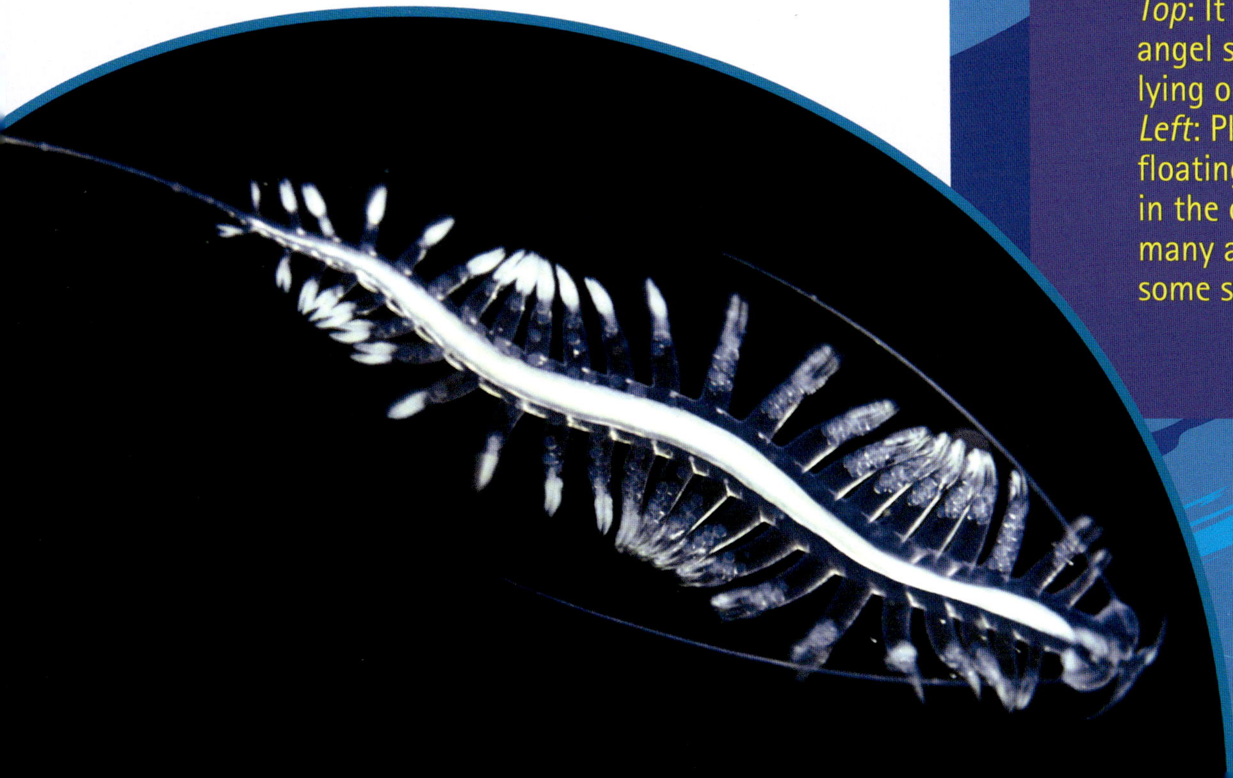

Top: It is hard to see an angel shark when it is lying on the ocean floor. *Left*: Plankton is tiny floating plant or animal life in the ocean. It is food for many animals, including some sharks.

All Kinds of Babies

Most fish give birth to their young by laying eggs. Different kinds of sharks give birth to their **pups** in different ways, though! Some sharks give birth to live young. Other sharks lay eggs on the ocean floor.

Top: The zebra shark lays eggs. *Left*: Hammerhead sharks give birth to live young.

In other sharks, the females lay eggs that hatch while they are still inside their bodies. Great white sharks and mako sharks give birth this way. The pups do not get food from their mothers' bodies. To survive, they will sometimes eat their brothers and sisters!

The great white shark's pups hatch from eggs while they are inside the mother's body.

Life Cycle of a Shark

1 Baby sharks are called pups. They swim away from their mothers as soon as they are born.

Shark Egg

4 Sharks give birth in one of three ways:

- Some sharks lay eggs in the ocean.
- Some sharks give birth to live young.
- Some sharks lay eggs that hatch inside their bodies. When the babies are big enough, they leave their mothers' bodies.

2

As they get older, sharks learn to use their senses of hearing, smell, and sight to hunt for their food.

3

Some small sharks are fully grown when they are just a few years old.

Some bigger sharks will not be fully grown until they are much older.

Pups

When a shark pup is born, it is much smaller than its mother. It has a full set of teeth, though, and it is ready to take care of itself. Right after birth, a pup will swim away from its mother. If it does not, she may decide to eat it!

Many pups will not survive their first year of life. Small sharks, such as the spined

Here is a young whitetip reef shark resting in a coral reef.

pygmy shark, are often eaten by bigger sharks. Even young great white sharks, which will be strong **predators** when they are older, must avoid being eaten by adult sharks.

These are young blacktip reef sharks. Like whitetip reef sharks, blacktip reef sharks swim in clear, shallow waters.

Growing Up

As young sharks grow, they become more like their parents. When a great white shark is born, it is generally around 5 feet (1.5 m) long. Within a few years, it will be closer to 15 feet (5 m) long! It will also eat different things. Young great whites eat mostly fish and rays. As they grow, they learn how to hunt larger animals.

Young great white sharks often hunt rays, like the manta ray shown here.

When great hammerhead sharks are born, their heads are rounder than those of their parents. As they grow, their heads will become more hammer shaped. They can then use their heads to trap stingrays on the ocean floor.

Adult great white sharks hunt seals, dolphins, and large fish like tuna.

Time to Mate

When sharks are fully grown, they are ready to **mate**, or have babies of their own. Many large sharks will not be ready to mate until they are between 10 and 17 years old. Some types of sharks, such as the great white, will have between 2 and 12 pups at a time. Other sharks, such as the blue shark, can give birth to nearly 100 pups at once!

Blue sharks are ready to mate when they are about five years old. The females give birth to live young.

Most sharks live between 20 and 30 years. Some can live much longer, though. The spiny dogfish can live up to 70 years!

The spiny dogfish has been known to live for 70 years. Most spiny dogfish live 30 to 40 years, though.

Our Ocean Friends

Many sharks live deep in the ocean and away from people. However, almost 100 species of sharks are in danger from people. This is mostly because of overfishing. Some sharks are caught by mistake when people use large nets or hooks to catch other fish. Other sharks are killed for their fins, which are eaten in some parts of the world.

This hammerhead shark has been caught in a fishing net by mistake.

With fewer sharks in the water, other species of fish may become too plentiful. This can hurt the balance of the oceans. Keeping all kinds of sharks safe is one way to keep the oceans of the world healthy.

Glossary

brackish (BRA-kish) Somewhat salty.

carnivores (KAHR-neh-vorz) Animals that eat other animals.

cartilage (KAHR-tuh-lij) The bendable matter from which people's noses and ears are made.

life cycle (LYF SY-kul) The different stages in an animal's life, from birth to death.

mate (MAYT) To come together to make babies.

mollusks (MAH-lusks) Animals without backbones and with soft bodies and, often, shells.

plankton (PLANK-ten) Plants and animals that drift with water currents.

predators (PREH-duh-terz) Animals that kill other animals for food.

pups (PUPS) Types of baby animals.

species (SPEE-sheez) One kind of living thing. All people are one species.

Index

Web Sites

Due to the changing nature of Internet links, PowerKids Press has developed an online list of Web sites related to the subject of this book. This site is updated regularly. Please use this link to access the list:
www.powerkidslinks.com/livl/shark/